Thank you for using your library

Earth

Stuart Clark

www.heinemann.co.uk/library
Visit our website to find out more information about **Heinemann Library** books.

To order:
☎ Phone 44 (0) 1865 888066
📄 Send a fax to 44 (0) 1865 314091
💻 Visit the Heinemann Bookshop at www.heinemann.co.uk/library to browse our catalogue and order online.

First published in Great Britain by Heinemann Library, Halley Court, Jordan Hill, Oxford OX2 8EJ, part of Harcourt Education. Heinemann is a registered trademark of Harcourt Education Ltd.

Editorial: Nick Hunter and Catherine Clarke
Design: Jo Hinton-Malivoire and AMR
Illustrations: Art Construction
Picture Research: Maria Joannou and Debra Weatherley
Production: Viv Hichens

Originated by Dot Gradations Ltd
Printed in Hong Kong, China by Wing King Tong

ISBN 0 431 15450 3
06 05 04 03 02
10 9 8 7 6 5 4 3 2 1

British Library Cataloguing in Publication Data
Clark, Stuart (Stuart G.)
  Earth. – (The universe)
  525
A full catalogue record for this book is available from the British Library.

Acknowledgements
The publishers would like to thank the following for permission to reproduce photographs: Getty Images p. **9**; NASA pp. **4**, **5**, **18**; Natural History Museum p. **26**; Science Photo Library pp. **10**, **11**, **13**, **14**, **15**, **16**, **20**, **23** (top and bottom), **24**, **25**, **27**, **28**; Still Pictures (Bill O'Connor) p. **29**; The Flight Collection p. **12**.

Cover photograph reproduced with permission of Photodisc.

Every effort has been made to contact copyright holders of any material reproduced in this book. Any omissions will be rectified in subsequent printings if notice is given to the publishers.

Contents

What does Earth look like from space?   4

Why does Earth have seasons?   8

Why can we breathe on Earth?   10

How high is the sky?   12

What is Earth's surface like?   14

What is Earth made of?   16

How was Earth made?   18

When did life begin on Earth?   24

Fact file   28

Glossary   30

Further reading   31

Index   32

Any words appearing in the text in bold, **like this**, are explained in the Glossary.

What does Earth look like from space?

The **planet** we live on is called Earth. From space, it looks like a giant, coloured ball. Earth is mostly blue because a lot of our planet is covered in water. These are the seas and oceans. The land is coloured brown and green and split up into **continents**. The North and South **Poles** are covered in white ice. Clouds drift around Earth.

This picture shows the planet Earth from space.

This picture shows all of the nine planets of our solar system, from Mercury to Pluto. Can you see Earth?

Our solar system

Earth is one of nine planets that **orbit** the Sun. Earth is the third planet from the Sun. Mercury and Venus are both closer. Mars, Jupiter, Saturn, Uranus, Neptune and Pluto are all further away. The Sun gives out light and warmth. The closer a planet is to the Sun, the hotter it will be. There are also billions of small objects, just a few kilometres across, that orbit the Sun. These are the rocky **asteroids** and the icy **comets**. Together, the Sun, the planets and all the smaller objects are called the **solar system**.

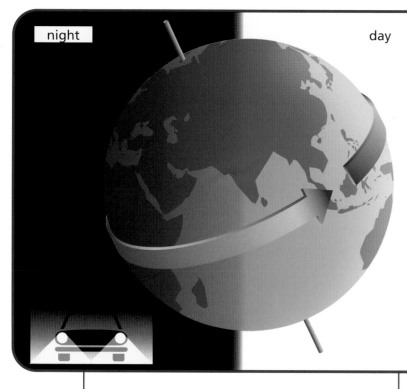

night

day

*Because Earth is always spinning on its **axis**, while one side is facing the Sun (and has day) the other is in darkness (and has night).*

Day and night

Standing on Earth, it looks as if the Sun climbs in the sky in the morning, travels across the sky and drops below the **horizon** at night. In fact, the Sun does not actually move through space. Instead, Earth spins slowly, making it look as if everything moves across the sky. As Earth spins, it shows different sides to the Sun. For the side of Earth facing the Sun, it is daytime. At the same time on the other side of Earth, it is night. It takes 24 hours for Earth to spin around once.

What shape is Earth?

Earth is shaped like a ball. So are all the other planets. It is said that some ancient people thought Earth was flat and if they travelled far enough towards the horizon, they would fall off the edge of the world! Anyone who watched a ship sail away knew this was not true. Instead of falling suddenly, the ship slowly disappeared below the horizon. This proves that Earth's surface slowly curves downwards, like the surface of a ball.

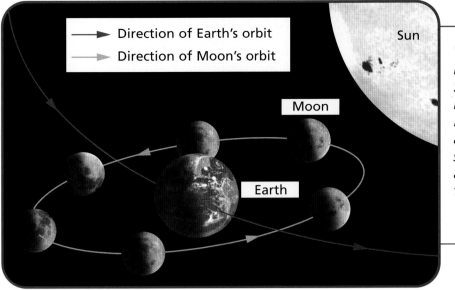

Direction of Earth's orbit
Direction of Moon's orbit

Sun

Moon

Earth

While Earth moves around the Sun, the Moon moves around Earth. Both Earth and the Moon are spinning on their axis at the same time as this.

Earth force

Earth has **gravity**. This is the force that keeps us on the ground. Gravity also stops the air we breathe from floating off into space. The **Moon** is caught in the gravity of Earth but is moving so fast that, instead of falling to Earth, it travels around it.

It takes about one month for the Moon to travel around our planet. During that time, the Moon always shows us the same face. Dark markings on the Moon are very old lava flows from **volcanic eruptions**.

How was Earth named?

The name Earth comes from **Old English** and German. It was being used before the year 1150. It is the only planet in the solar system whose English name is not based on Greek and Roman **mythology**. To the Romans, the Earth goddess was called Tellus, meaning fertile soil. The Greeks called her Gaia.

Why does Earth have seasons?

Earth follows a circular path around the Sun called an **orbit**. All the other **planets** in the **solar system** also orbit the Sun. It takes Earth one year to travel all the way around its orbit. During that time, Earth goes through four seasons: spring, summer, autumn and winter.

Going for a spin

As Earth moves through its orbit, it also spins on its **axis**. The axis is an imaginary line that runs from the North **Pole**, through the centre of Earth, to the South Pole. Earth's axis is tilted. Instead of pointing straight up, it has been knocked over to the side a little. When the North Pole is leaning towards the Sun, it is summer in the north.

Six months later, Earth has moved half way around its orbit and the North Pole is now leaning away from the Sun. When this happens, it is winter in the north. When the North Pole is leaning away from the Sun, the South Pole is leaning towards the Sun. So, when it is winter in the north, it is summer in the south.

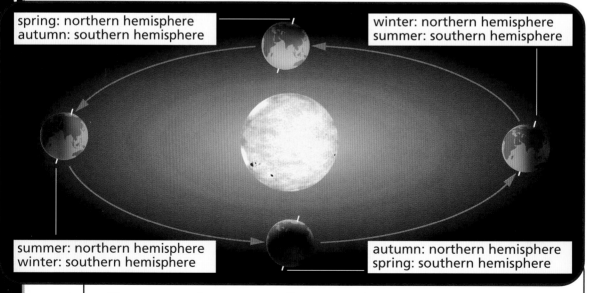

spring: northern hemisphere
autumn: southern hemisphere

winter: northern hemisphere
summer: southern hemisphere

summer: northern hemisphere
winter: southern hemisphere

autumn: northern hemisphere
spring: southern hemisphere

The seasons change according to Earth's position in its orbit around the Sun.

This series of photos were taken over a period of 24 hours, in Norway, near the Arctic Circle, during the summer. Even at midnight (sixth picture from the left) the Sun does not go below the horizon and therefore, there is no 'night'.

Night for three months

During the northern winter, the North Pole is tilted so far away from the Sun that the Sun never rises above the **horizon**. It is night there for three whole months. The same thing happens at the South Pole six months later. When it is summer in the north, the Sun stays in the sky above the North Pole so it is daylight for three whole months. Again, this happens at the South Pole six months later, when it is summer there.

Not all places on Earth have spring, summer, autumn and winter. The **equator** is an imaginary line around the middle of Earth, halfway between the North and South Poles. The area near the equator is known as the **tropics**. In the tropics, it is hot all the time. Some places have a wet season when it rains a lot. At other times of the year, it is very dry. Many deserts are found near the equator. This is where the temperatures are hottest and there is very little rain.

Why can we breathe on Earth?

Earth is covered with a thin blanket of **gases**, called the **atmosphere**. The special mixture of gases in Earth's atmosphere is called air. Although many other **planets** have their own atmospheres, no other planet in the **solar system** has an atmosphere with the mixture of gases we call air. So it would be impossible for humans to breathe on the other planets. If astronauts land on other worlds, they will need to wear spacesuits.

Earth's atmosphere

The special gas in the air that we breathe is called oxygen. We need oxygen to change the food we eat into the energy we need to live. Nearly all living things need oxygen to stay alive. Fires need oxygen to burn, too. Not all our atmosphere is oxygen. Most of it is a gas called nitrogen. Nitrogen puts fires out. If there were more oxygen in our atmosphere and less nitrogen, fires would burn faster and spread more quickly.

The clouds we see in the sky are part of Earth's atmosphere. If you were standing at the top of one of these mountains, in South America, the clouds and mist would be all around you.

This picture shows Earth from space. You can clearly see the layer of atmosphere that covers Earth's surface. There are clouds in the atmosphere.

The atmosphere is held around Earth by **gravity**. Some planets do not have atmospheres. This is because they are too small to make enough gravity to hold onto the gases. Instead, the gases float off into space.

How does Earth's atmosphere protect us?

The atmosphere does a lot more than just give us air to breathe. It acts like a blanket, keeping our planet warm. It also blocks out harmful **radiation** from space called cosmic rays. When astronauts spend a long time in space, their spacecraft must have a special room with very thick walls to protect them from cosmic rays. An alarm tells the astronauts when to shelter because the number of cosmic rays has become dangerous. A special layer in our atmosphere, called the ozone layer, also blocks most of the **ultraviolet** light from the Sun. In small amounts, ultraviolet light will give you a suntan but large amounts can make people very ill and can cause skin cancer.

How high is the sky?

What we think of as the sky above our heads is actually Earth's **atmosphere**. The atmosphere stretches about 200 kilometres (just over 125 miles) above the ground. Although that sounds a lot, it is only about the distance a car travels in a few hours. As you get higher up, the atmosphere becomes thinner. This means there are less gases, including oxygen, around you. So, it gets more difficult to breathe.

The tallest mountain on Earth is Mount Everest. It rises almost 9 kilometres (almost 5.6 miles) into the sky. At the top of the mountain the air is so thin that most people who climb the mountain have to wear masks to give them extra oxygen so that they can breathe.

Flying above the clouds

Jet aircraft fly at about 10 kilometres (about 6 miles) above the ground. This is the highest that people can travel, unless they are astronauts – going into space. Most clouds form between 2 kilometres (about 1 and a half miles) and 5 kilometres (about 3 miles) above the ground. There are many different types of cloud and scientists study them to help predict the weather.

This jet is high up in the atmosphere. At this height you can see how Earth's **horizon** *curves.*

Burn up

Entering Earth's atmosphere can make things burn up. Sometimes, bright darts of light shoot across the sky. These are called shooting stars but they are not really stars. They are tiny pieces of space dust coming towards Earth. They fly through space very quickly. When they hit the atmosphere they become very hot and burn up because of friction. Friction is what makes your hands warm when you rub them together.

Spacecraft

The lowest spacecraft **orbit** Earth at 515 kilometres (322 miles). Sometimes Earth's gravity pulls them down. Like shooting stars, they hit the atmosphere and burn up. In 2001, the Russians destroyed their old **space station**, called *Mir*, like this. They used a spacecraft to push it on to a **collision course** with Earth's atmosphere. The heat burnt up most of the space station but not all of it. It was so big that some of it survived and fell into the Pacific Ocean.

This artwork shows how the Space Shuttle does not burn up when it re-enters the atmosphere because it is covered in heat-proof tiles.

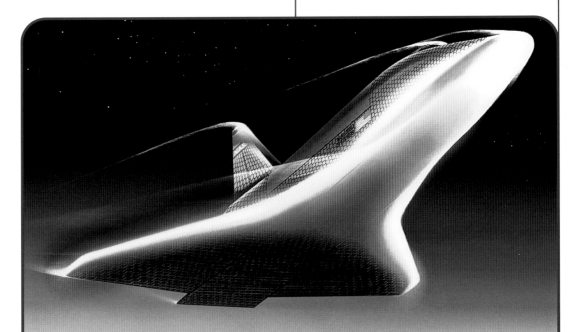

What is Earth's surface like?

Land and oceans cover Earth's surface. There are many different types of land. Some parts are covered with jungles, others with snow. There are rugged mountains and hot, sandy deserts.

The oceans are very special. They are Earth's central heating system. They help warm up the cooler parts of the **planet**. In some houses, hot water is pumped around the radiators to keep the rooms warm. On Earth, warm water moves around the oceans, keeping some countries warmer than others.

*Earth has all sorts of weather. Storms in the **tropics** have very strong winds and produce huge amounts of rain.*

The right distance from the Sun

Earth is very different from all the other planets in the **solar system**. It is the only one that has animals and plants living on it. This is because our planet is just the right distance from the Sun.

If Earth were closer to the Sun, it would be so hot that the water would boil away. If Earth were too far away from the Sun, it would be so cold that the oceans would freeze into solid ice. Without water, life on Earth would be impossible.

*Factories and power stations that burn **fossil fuels** are adding to the pollution in our atmosphere.*

Is Earth's climate changing?

Scientists are now very worried that Earth's **climate** is changing. For more than 20 years, Earth has been getting hotter. Part of this change is natural. Throughout Earth's history temperatures have been changing slightly. However, some of the present change is being caused by pollution. This is waste **gas** from cars and factories. The pollution hangs in the **atmosphere** and acts like a blanket on a bed, keeping in heat. If we continue to make pollution, Earth will become too hot for us to live.

What is Earth made of?

Earth is made mostly of rocks. The rocks are made of many different **chemicals**. Scientists called **geologists** study rocks. When geologists know what a rock is made of, they can work out how it was formed. There are three different types of rock on Earth. These rocks make up the surface. The surface of Earth is called the **crust** and is usually between 10 and 50 kilometres thick. In some parts under the oceans it can be much thinner.

Different layers

The first type of rock is called **igneous rock**. This makes up most of Earth's surface and was once **molten lava**. The lava

erupts from **volcanoes** and then cools down to become rock. The second type of rock is called **sedimentary rock**. This is made of little bits of sand and other small pieces that drift to the bottom of the sea. As more bits fall on top, the tiny pieces are squashed together and become rock. The third type is called **metamorphic rock**. This is made from igneous or sedimentary rocks that have been squeezed or heated inside Earth and turned into different rocks.

You can see the different layers in this sedimentary rock along the coast of the Isle of Wight, UK.

16

Inside Earth

Geologists can use special equipment to listen to sounds travelling through Earth. It is a good way to discover far away **earthquakes** and volcanic eruptions and is called **seismology**. It also helps scientists discover what chemicals make up Earth. When scientists first listened to the inside of Earth, they found that at the very centre of our planet is a large ball of metal. It is mostly made of iron and nickel. At the centre of the ball the metal is solid, but near the surface the metal is so hot that it is molten.

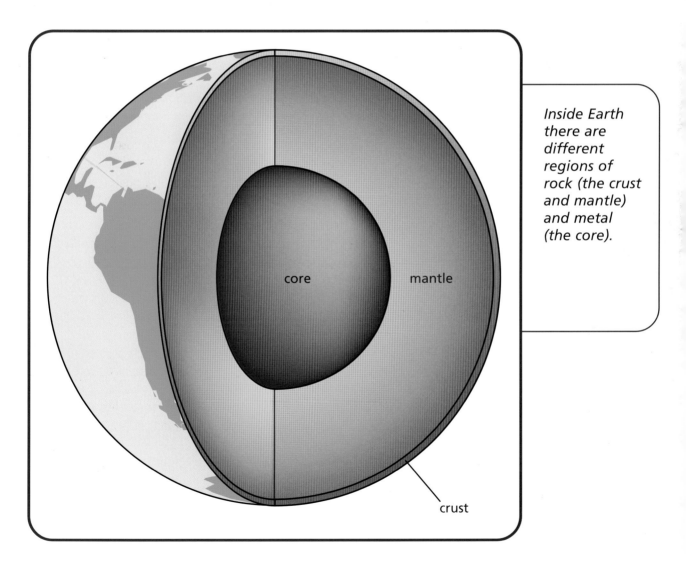

core

mantle

crust

Inside Earth there are different regions of rock (the crust and mantle) and metal (the core).

How was Earth made?

Geologists are very good at measuring the different types of **chemicals** that make up the rocks on Earth. By weighing the amount of each chemical inside a rock, scientists can measure how old it is. Using this method to find the oldest rocks on Earth, geologists have worked out that Earth is 4.5 billion years old.

Astronomers have worked out the age of the Sun. It is also 4.5 billion years old. This tells us that Earth, the Sun and all the **planets** formed at the same time. A big clue about how Earth was formed can be found in space.

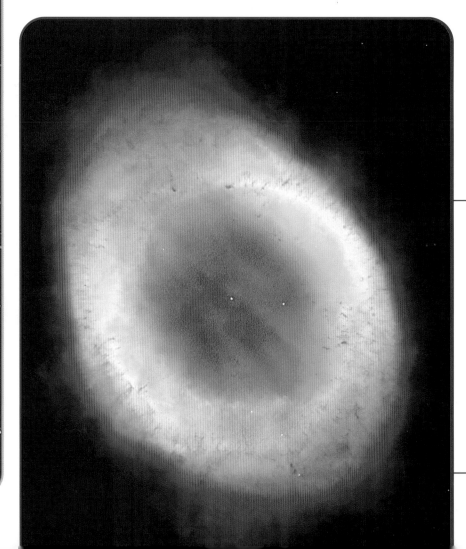

This brightly coloured cloud of gas and dust is called a 'planetary nebula'. Scientists have discovered that planets are made inside clouds like this.

Clouds in space

When astronomers look into space, they see enormous clouds of gas and dust. Some of the clouds reflect light, giving off beautiful red, yellow and green colours. The clouds are much bigger than planets or stars. Using telescopes to look inside them, astronomers can see that stars form inside these clouds. Planets must form inside them, too.

Star making

As the clouds float through space, parts of them begin to move closer together. This is the first step in making a star. As the gas squeezes together, it heats up and becomes a star. Small clouds of dust then form around these very young stars. This is where astronomers think planets form. So, stars and planets form together, at the same time, and this is how scientists think our **solar system** was made.

Planets forming

No one has ever seen a forming planet. Telescopes are not powerful enough to see any detail in the dusty clouds that surround young stars. Astronomers are working to build bigger telescopes that will see into the clouds. Until those telescopes are finished, astronomers have to rely on very powerful computers to help them calculate what happens when a planet forms. They believe it takes many millions of years for a planet to form completely.

Their calculations tell them that the dust in the cloud begins to stick together. This takes a long time. After many, many thousands of years, the dust sticks together to make rocks. Then, the rocks start to bump into each other. When this happens, they melt and stick together. As more of the rocks stick together, they form planets, and this is how scientists think Earth was made.

This crater is in Arizona, USA. It is huge – 800 metres wide and 200 metres deep.

Craters

Most of the rocks have come together, over millions of years, to make planets but there are still some rocks that have not. The **craters** on the Moon were caused as these last pieces of rock were caught by **gravity** and crashed into the Moon's surface. There would have been many craters on Earth too but most of them have been worn away by the weather.

The restless Earth

Even today, the temperature inside Earth is high and some of the rocks are still **molten**. This is called **magma** and it behaves like a liquid. The surface of Earth is not one solid **crust**. Instead it is broken into large pieces called plates. The plates hold the **continents** and the oceans and they float on the magma. As the liquid magma moves, so do the plates. Sometimes they collide. Other times they pull apart. When plates rub along each other, **earthquakes** happen. These shake the ground and cause awful damage. The plate containing the Pacific Ocean rubs against the west coast of the USA, creating terrible earthquakes from time to time. If continents collide, the plates can push up into mountain ranges. This is happening at the moment where India is pushing into Asia, creating the Himalayan mountain range.

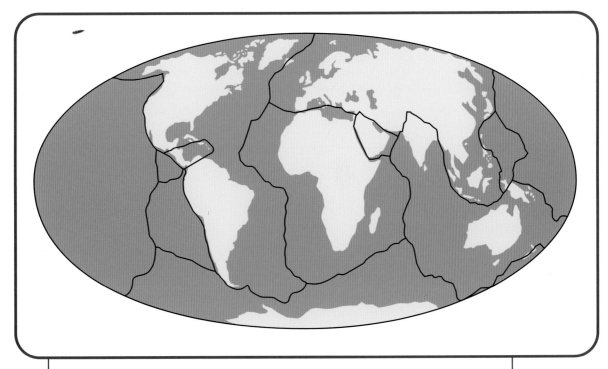

Earth's crust fits together like a jigsaw puzzle. The pieces are called plates. Wherever two plates meet, or touch, there is a risk of earthquakes.

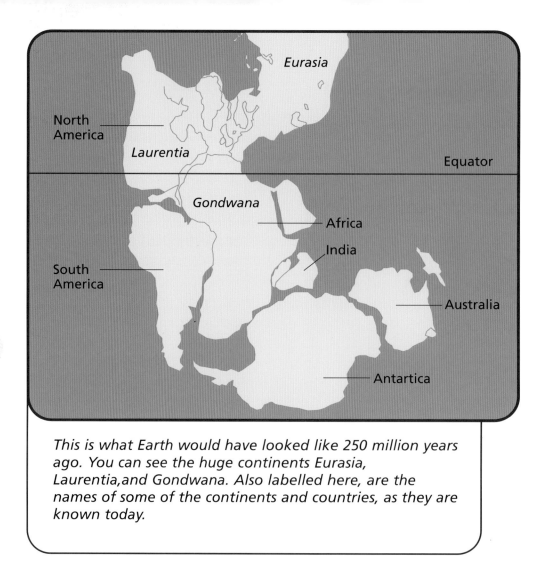

This is what Earth would have looked like 250 million years ago. You can see the huge continents Eurasia, Laurentia,and Gondwana. Also labelled here, are the names of some of the continents and countries, as they are known today.

One enormous continent

Most of the land on Earth was once a single enormous **continent**. It split apart 250 million years ago and the pieces have taken all of that time to drift into their present positions. South America looks as though it would fit into Africa like a jigsaw puzzle because once, long ago, they were joined together.

Volcanic eruptions

Magma can also rise to the surface of Earth and **erupt**, through holes that become **volcanoes**. When magma flows out of Earth it is called **lava**. As it hardens and turns into new rock, it builds large volcanoes.

It is very difficult to know when a volcano will erupt. There can be many years or even decades between **volcanic eruptions**. A volcano is said to be 'dormant' when it is not erupting. When it stops erupting altogether, a volcano is said to be 'extinct'.

Some volcanos erupt violently, with explosions and huge clouds of ash. Others erupt gently with flowing lava and no explosions.

Changing Earth

There were times in the past when Earth was much colder than it is today. These times are called ice ages. Huge sheets of ice creep over the land and gigantic icebergs float on the oceans. Ice ages may be caused when extremely large volcanoes erupt. They throw clouds of ash into the **atmosphere** and stop sunlight from reaching Earth. The temperature of our planet would then drop and an ice age would happen.

When did life begin on Earth?

Fossils are made when parts of dead animals or plants leave marks in **sedimentary rocks**. Scientists have found very old fossils in some rocks. These fossils are amazing because they are not like the large bones of dinosaurs. Instead, they are very tiny fossils of **bacteria**. These are the smallest life forms found on Earth and can only be seen through a microscope. There are many different types of bacteria. Nowadays, some bacteria give us illnesses, while others live inside us and help us to digest our food. The rocks in which fossils of old bacteria have been found are 3.5 billion years old.

Other scientists have found rocks almost 4 billion years old that were probably made from dead bacteria. So, it seems that bacteria were the first life forms on Earth. No one knows exactly how bacteria formed in the first place. This is one of the most puzzling questions in modern science.

Some of these ammonite fossils are around 380 million years old. Ammonites were a type of sea snail.

Plants and animals

For nearly 3 billion years, bacteria were the only kind of life that lived on Earth and they were only found in the oceans. Then, 600 million years ago, life on Earth suddenly changed. Groups of bacteria stuck together and worked together, becoming more complicated. Plants and animals developed. The first plants were like vines and the first animals were like jellyfish. Eventually both plants and animals found ways to leave the ocean and to live on the land.

Mass extinction

Animals and plants change all the time. Usually they become more and more complicated. This change is called 'evolution', and it means that animals and plants can adapt to new situations. One mystery that is still to be solved by scientists is why certain types of animals die out suddenly. When this happens it is called a **mass extinction**. There have been five mass extinctions during Earth's history.

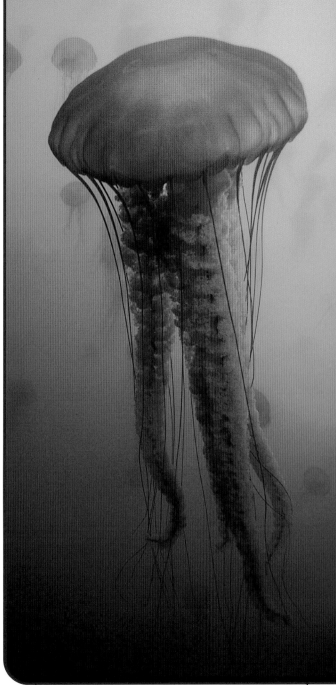

Simple creatures, like this jellyfish, were some of the first animals to develop on Earth.

Death of the dinosaurs

A very important **mass extinction** took place 65 million years ago. This was when the last of the dinosaurs died out suddenly. The dinosaurs were giant animals that lived on Earth between 225 and 65 million years ago. Most scientists believe that they were finally wiped out when a gigantic lump of space rock, known as an **asteroid**, hit Earth. An asteroid is often the size of a mountain and if it crashes into a planet it will cause powerful **earthquakes** and **volcanoes** will **erupt**. These terrible disasters probably killed the dinosaurs and a large number of other animals and plants. Scientists have found evidence that the other mass extinctions may also have been caused by asteroids.

This Shunosaurus dinosaur skeleton was found in China. The Shunosaurus was a plant-eating dinosaur, so even if it had survived the impact of the asteroid, it would probably have starved with no plants left to eat.

The birth of man

The extinction of the dinosaurs is important to us because, after the death of these huge creatures there was more food for the smaller creatures called **mammals**. Mammals began to **evolve** about 210 million years ago. They give birth to live babies rather than laying eggs. They also feed their babies with milk. Humans are highly developed mammals. Most scientists believe that humans evolved from earlier, simpler mammals. The first mammals evolved to become more complicated and more intelligent. After millions of years they finally became human beings.

This is an artist's idea of what early humans would have looked like around 1 million years ago.

Can we stop asteroids hitting Earth?

There is always a small risk that another asteroid might hit Earth. **Astronomers** are building new telescopes and searching the skies for dangerous asteroids. If such an asteroid is discovered, instead of blowing it up, scientists will try to push it into a new **orbit** so it will not crash into Earth.

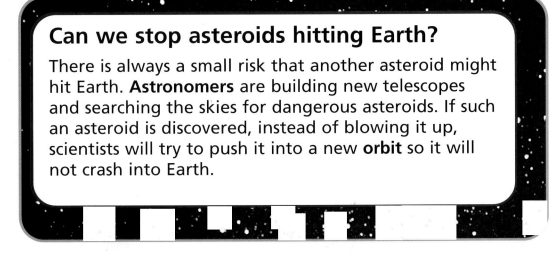

Fact file

While one half of Earth is in sunlight and has day, the other half is in darkness and has night.

Earth

Length of day – 24 hours

Distance from Sun – 150 million kilometres (93 million miles)

Time to go around the Sun – 365.25 days (So every fourth year we have to include an extra day in the calendar, 29 February. These are known as leap years. If we did not do this, the seasons would shift out of order with the months of the year.)

Size – Earth is 12750 kilometres (7968 miles) across

Surface area – The surface of Earth measures 510 million square kilometres (196 million square miles)

Average height of the land – 840 metres above sea level

Average depth of the oceans – 3800 metres
Earth's atmosphere is made of:

The five tallest mountains:
Mount Everest	8.8 kilometres (5.5 miles)
Godwin Austen (K2)	8.6 kilometres (5.4 miles)
Kanchenjunga	8.59 kilometres (5.33 miles)
Lhotse	8.5 kilometres (5.3 miles)
Makalu	8.5 kilometres (5.3 miles)

The Himalayan mountain range is the highest in the world. It is constantly covered in snow and nothing lives on the mountain peaks.

The five longest rivers:
Nile	6670 kilometres (4145 miles)
Amazon	6430 kilometres (4000 miles)
Yangtze	6300 kilometres (3915 miles)
Mississippi	6020 kilometres (3741 miles)
Yenisei-Angara	5540 kilometres (3442 miles)

Earth's atmosphere is made of:
Nitrogen gas	78 per cent
Oxygen gas	21 per cent
Argon gas	0.9 per cent
All other gases	0.1 per cent

Glossary

asteroid small object orbiting the Sun. Some are just lumps of rock in space. Others are many kilometres wide.

astronomers scientists who study space, planets and stars

atmosphere blanket of gas around a planet or moon

axis imaginary line that a planet spins around

bacteria tiny, basic life forms

chemicals substances that everything is made up from

climate weather conditions

collision course about to hit or crash into something

comet body of rock and ice travelling around the Sun

continent very large piece of land on Earth. Europe is a continent.

crater large, bowl-shaped hole in the surface of a planet or moon caused by an asteroid crashing into it

crust outer layer of Earth – all the continents and oceans sit on the crust

earthquake when the surface of Earth moves suddenly

equator imaginary line around the middle of Earth

erupt burst out

evolve change over time

gas substance like air

geologists scientists who study rocks

gravity force that pulls all objects towards the surface of Earth, or any other planet, moon or star

horizon line where the land and the sky seem to meet

igneous rocks rocks made from lava

lava liquid rock that erupts from volcanoes

magma rocks that are so hot they are liquid and runny

mammals animals that give birth to babies and feed them with milk – humans are mammals

mass extinction when a type of animal dies out forever

metamorphic rocks rocks changed by heat or squeezing

molten something that has been melted

Moon, the natural satellite that orbits Earth. Astronauts first went there in 1969.

mythology old stories, told to explain how something came to be

Old English language people in England used to speak before the year 1150 – it is different from the English we speak now

orbit path one object takes around another

planet large object that orbits a star – Earth is a planet

Poles two points – one at each end of Earth's axis – the North Pole and the South Pole

radiation energy rays from the Sun

sedimentary rocks rocks made up over time from tiny bits

seismology special way of listening for, and studying, earthquakes

solar system all the planets, moons, asteroids and comets around the Sun

space station large man-made object that orbits Earth – astronauts can live on it

tropics area of Earth around the equator

ultraviolet light special light that cannot be seen by humans. Ultraviolet light from the Sun causes skin to tan, and can cause cancer.

volcanic eruptions active volcanos that spill lava on to the Earth's surface

volcano opening in a planet's surface through which hot, liquid rock is thrown up

Further reading

Earth and Moon, Robin Kerrod and David Atkinson (Belitha Press, 2000)
Eyewitness Guides: Earth, Suzanna Van Rose (Dorling Kindersley, 1998)
How the universe works, Heather Couper and Nigel Henbest (Dorling Kindersley, 1999)

Index

age of Earth 18
asteroids 5, 26, 27
atmosphere 10, 11, 12, 13, 15, 23, 29

bacteria 24, 25

climate change 15
clouds and rain 4, 10, 11, 12
comets 5
continents 4, 21, 22
craters 20
crust 16, 17, 21

day and night 6, 9, 28

dinosaurs 26

earthquakes 17, 21, 26
equator 9
evolution 25, 27

fossils 24

gravity 7, 11, 13, 20

ice ages 23
igneous rock 16

life on Earth 14, 24–27

magma 21, 22
metamorphic rock 16
meteors 13

Moon 7, 20
mountains 12, 21, 29

North and South Poles 4, 8, 9

oceans 4, 14, 21, 28
orbit 5, 7, 8, 13, 27
oxygen 10, 12
ozone layer 11

planets 4, 5, 6, 8, 10, 14, 18, 19
pollution 15

radiation 11

seasons 8, 9
sedimentary rock 16, 24
seismology 17
shooting stars 13
size and shape of Earth 6, 28
solar systems 5, 8, 10, 14, 19
spacecraft 11, 13
stars 19
Sun 5, 6, 8, 9, 14, 18, 28
surface of Earth 14, 16, 21

temperature of Earth 15, 21, 23
tropics 9, 14

ultraviolet light 11

volcanic eruptions 7, 16, 22–23, 26